MW00695752

If you have ever been a caregiver for a loved one in the past, or if you are one in the present or will be one in the future, I encourage you to read *Care and Prayer* by Gunilla Norris. Ms. Norris takes a compassionate view of the role of the caregiver and brings spirituality and love to the subject. Utilizing prayer in the form of poetry to convey her message, Ms. Norris shows readers that caregiving is the ultimate act of love and kindness.

It is important to the author that the reader be changed by the book. As a reader myself, I can say that she has succeeded.

JAMES SCARLES, MD

Caregiving is indeed a sacred and holy task, because it is based on the Scripture, "whatever you do to one of these you do to me."

Each chapter is a little soundbite to keep one focused on their "yes," their desire to be with another, and therefore with THE OTHER. Then caregiving is elevated to a transformative level.

Once again Gunilla Norris cuts to the heart of the matter.

FATHER CARL ARICO, *founding member of*
Contemplative Outreach, priest of the Archdiocese of Newark,
and author of **A Taste of Silence**

Parkinson's disease is a chronic progressive neurodegenerative disorder with no cure. Cold clinical words do not even begin to capture the life that Stan and Gunilla lived for over 20 years.

Most people can appreciate the inner strength and compassion of someone who takes on the role of caregiver, but to continue to love, even as this relentless condition erodes at everything they knew and cherished about the person they cared for, that takes true integrity.

Throughout this pensive collection of Gunilla's musings, the reader can feel her anguish, her desolation, her self-doubt. But for every page that reveals her pain, she calls on her strong sense of self and her faith in God on the immediate page following. "Cradle me, Lord....Let receiving your healing love be what I pass on to those for whom I care."

Ultimately, she shares with all of us her complete confidence that her caregiving role was simply the fulfillment of her destiny toward self-actualization and one-ness with God. And with this certitude, she bequeathed us peace.

J. **Antonelle de Marcaida, MD,** *medical director,*
Hartford HealthCare, Chase Family Movement Disorders Center

CARE
AND
PRAYER

Reflections
on the Sacred Task
of Caregiving

GUNILLA NORRIS

**TWENTY-THIRD
PUBLICATIONS**
twentythirdpublications.com

TWENTY-THIRD PUBLICATIONS
One Montauk Avenue, Suite 200
New London, CT 06320
(860) 437-3012 or (800) 321-0411
www.twentythirdpublications.com

Cover photo: ©Shutterstock.com / fotohunter

ISBN: 978-1-62785-566-2
Printed in the U.S.A.

 A Division of Bayard, Inc.
Bayard CEO: Hugues de Foucauld

TABLE OF CONTENTS

NOTE TO THE READER

This is not a book to read from cover to cover. You shouldn't. It's a book to dip into when you sense you would like to read about something that could help you in your caregiving. The giving of care is often lonely, and so to have a book that will act as a friend to you might be just what is needed.

Keep it by your bed, in the bathroom, or on the kitchen counter. It can even be in the car when you might have found a minute by the roadside or while waiting at the doctor's office. This book is for you to pick up spontaneously. Read it on the fly. It's probably the only way you can read these days. Or read it on those rare occasions when you have time and can mull. I hope you will feel that you are not alone in the depth of the very difficult task you find yourself in. In the end, the answers and solace you hunger for will come from your own wisdom. We each have to work out the meaning of our lives. To pray about that is natural. After every reflection you will find a little prayer that hopefully will inspire you to pray in your own way and so find *your* way as the days unfold.

I wrote this book to be in solidarity with you. The task is daunting. The regrets and mistakes made on the way will probably haunt us long after we are done. No one person is ever enough for another's needs, and yet we have to do our best and forgive our failures as we go. We will never regret that we took up this difficult path of love and followed through with it. May this little book be of use and blessing to you.

If you can find a path with no obstacles, it probably doesn't lead anywhere.

Frank A. Clark

INTRODUCTION

A book is not alive without its readers. Thank you for making this book come alive in some way that I will never know. For me that is a good mystery, and one I will never want to solve.

As a writer the inspiration for a book happens in many ways. Perhaps a powerful image or experience prompts the writing. Sometimes a need to address something important or difficult arises. Mostly ideas come and then leave—out of the mind and out the door. But some stick to you and demand to be taken seriously.

I was so through with caregiving. I never wanted to think about it ever again. I was a caregiver to my beloved partner, Stanley, for over ten years. He had Parkinson's disease. His body failed him little by little. His mind filled with dreadful hell states and a fierce distrust and anger toward the very person who was giving her all to him day after day. This, I later learned, is a very common symptom of Parkinson's disease. We know caregiving is not for sissies. We have to be present to what comes. It's like riding an escalator. We are moved relentlessly. Even though there may be plateaus, they don't last, for the escalator keeps going, and all we can do is to be fully on the step we are on and do, there, the best we can while we are moved from one level to the next.

I don't want to go into the details of what happened to me.* Instead, I trust that I never write a book alone. Circumstances, lived experiences, chance, conversations, wounds, and hopes are all there as inspirations— a crowd helping the process along. I have learned to be a willing servant to what wants to happen. Besides, a teasing angel at my shoulder was very irritating, and to comply with her insistence I had to write.

Then there is also *you*, the reader, to whom this book is addressed. I am reaching out to you in these reflections. The squiggles on a page amount to nothing without your eyes, your heart, your understanding, experience, and participation.

You will soon find out that this book is not a *how-to* book. I don't know enough to write such a book. There are hundreds of them dealing with memory loss, cancer, help for those who suffer from immune diseases, and so on. There are also books giving expert advice for caregivers on how to take care of themselves. What criteria, then, do I have to write about caregiving? Only this: I loved and suffered with my partner for ten years, coping with the relentless decline of Parkinson's disease. I was not a great caregiver. I made lots of mistakes, but I showed up, and I could not have done so without a prayer life. It is what sustained me.

As you read this book please also sense and join the vast numbers of people, past, present, and future, who are giving

---

*You can read about that in my two books of poetry: *Joy Is the Thinnest Layer* and *Calling the Creatures*.

or have given care. We are not alone in our journeys. We are part of the family of humanity, where helping one another is central to being human. It shapes who we become.

The giving of care is fraught with many things: love, responsibility, relentlessness, confusion, control, fatigue, anger, despair, humor, sadness, and God's presence throughout it all, if we would only sense it, and find that, as we love, we are also being loved.

Not everything on these pages will be relevant to you. May you be sustained as you live this holy task of giving care. Skip those parts that don't speak to you. Opening the book at random might work for you. The reflections are short on purpose. Caregivers have so little time! The prayers are even shorter, though one or two might reach into a place where Spirit can enter and be with you. They will then turn out to be long in both forming and transforming your heart. May you be supported and find tender, respectful ways to live, not just for the one you are caring for but for yourself as well.

I do not for a minute take you or your reading of this book for granted. It is you who will make this book come alive just as the ears of people at a concert make music felt and heard.

NOTES ON PRAYER

In my understanding, God has already given us everything in advance, an abundance of everything, and is never apart from us. When I pray, I don't think of trying to influence a God *out there somewhere* to do something for me. God is present right where I am whether I feel it or not.

Addressing God in prayer, then, is more a way to open me, to help me to receive God's love in whatever way my limited consciousness can. When I confess my longings, my failures, and my efforts as well as my needs and joys, I become more transparent. I can feel, then, that God is in relationship to me as I am in relationship to God. This is not magical hoping to be spared pain and suffering. It is more a growing experience of the bottomless compassion that God is, and so a desire to participate in that compassion emerges in the situations I find myself in.

I know that of my own self I can do nothing, but the love that has already been given to me in abundance can infuse me, change me, reassure me, and support me. The act of praying opens the door to my heart and to ways to live more faithfully and fruitfully.

We have the limitations of our bodies and our circumstances. But within them lie vast possibilities of acceptance and growth. We can learn to embody love, peace, forgiveness, and presence. For me, prayers are the keys that can help unlock our resistance and allow Spirit to govern and guide us.

The bigger picture will always be unknown to us, and yet we are intrinsic parts of that picture. I believe we can trust that the longing in our hearts will move us more and more into a companionship with God and so to those rightful places for us to live and serve.

We can write our prayers, sing our prayers, hum them, say them in silence, and reach out with hands and arms to move them as wordless expressions of our hearts. With prayer as a relationship, we are opened to an inner, living relationship with God in which many things become possible. To be in and about care is one of them.

CARE
AND
PRAYER

Invited into Life

We suffer a lot when the one or ones we care about are suffering. We also ache when our own emotional and physical challenges overwhelm us. It is very hard then to remember that God loves us. Those words become only words, even platitudes.

The truth is that the Old English meaning of the word *suffer* was *to allow*. When too much pain fills our lives and the lives of others, we can't feel that God's love is present. Our doors to love slam shut. We wonder where God is as we suffer.

It may seem impossible to understand that God's love is not a love that prevents suffering, but a love that joins in the unfolding of whatever is occurring. God suffers and rejoices in every one of us. God participates. There is no old, white Patriarch in the sky who points at us with a condemning finger. Instead, there is unlimited life, and the freedom to be in its unfolding. God's love is an allowing love. It asks us to take up our lives and unfold them with as much human care as we can muster. It is there, in the living, that meaning is to be found.

To love life is to accept that it cannot be controlled. It can only be lived. Allowing God's gift of possibility is to remember we are not facing what we face alone. As close as our next breath, God invites us into Life—the very one we are living now. Can we remember that immense gift as we suffer? To re*member* is to connect again, to become once more a *member* of Life itself just as it is and to God who can never be defined, but whom we can sense being near to us and suffering with us. We start there. We live there every moment. God never abandons what God created. We need daily to remember the truth of that.

When I falter and distrust,
when I ache and suffer
beyond what I think I can take, let me know
that here, in this frail human body
I am yet a member of Your body,
Your creation.

Let my mind be still
and the truth of your Presence be
what I come to know in my very cells.

May I not ask, "Why me?"
Instead may I be led to the tasks
that are truly mine to do.
May I remember Your love
and say, "Yes."

The Gaze of Love

In the tension, the slop, and the cleanup, the hurry and waiting, fearing and unknowing that fill a caregiving day, how can we possibly grasp that we are revered and precious? *Who me?* we might ask, sleeves pulled up, half-eaten sandwich on the table, dishes in the sink.

But if we could peer behind and under the veil of appearances, we might sense that infinite love is pouring into us and into what is all around us. Yes, that is a leap of faith, and that leap cannot happen without profound humility. It is the willingness to give up the veil of comfy, controlling self-assessments of how nice we are as well as the automatic, negative judgments about our selves and our situations.

Being willing to see behind the veil takes enormous guts. To let go of being right about our unworthiness or our self-serving goodness and how unfair life can seem to be: this will only happen in humility. To dare to believe that we are loved beyond anything that seems to prove otherwise is to be ego-reduced. It is an abject state in which we are not able to claim anything. And yet it is precisely there that God honors us. God loves our weakness and our need. That undeserved love is what can fuel us for the tasks at hand.

To claim and to be in this fundamental state of humility is perhaps the only way we can stay whole in the grief, hopelessness, and exhaustion that caregiving can become. We need practice. Before a mirror in our homes let us look into our own eyes. Can we simply look and not assess? Can the eyes that we see with just gaze at the one who stands there? Perhaps we can learn to baby-gaze. Infants and toddlers just look and experience, don't they? They have no pre-judgment. With curiosity and interest, they are taking in what is present. It is a kind of sacred gazing. If we can learn to do this as conscious adults we would be a step closer to knowing that we are already known in our strengths, our frailties, our faults, and our preciousness. There's nothing to hide and everything to gain. Can we let ourselves be naked and love-seen by God? Can we let ourselves be held dear?

How can I rid myself of the veils
with which I cover myself;
not being enough, not caring
as much as I think I should?

I dress myself in my oh so familiar
rain and storm gear—those negative opinions
of who I believe myself to be.

Sometimes I brag inside when no one can see it.
Look how good I am
as I demonstrate my care.

Secretly I want to believe
there is only this wonderful me
proving myself to everyone.

Your presence wants me naked to Your love.
Teach me humility. Help me give up
the sweet control
I find in self-assessment.
Help me unbutton and unzip.

The Inner *Yes*

The daily gift of being remembered into God's keeping and growing the humility of letting in, little by little, how much we are cherished and revered can change the course of our caregiving from one of dread and obligation to one of courage and acceptance.

It helps a great deal to acknowledge that caregiving is not bondage, but a holy task, one of service and dignity. It's true that caregivers are often taken for granted, left in the lurch with the whole catastrophe. They are often not thanked, and most likely they will be criticized for the ways they are handling things. Who would want such a job unless they were called to it?

Understood as a holy task, the job shows up with our

names on it. We can't avoid what belongs to us. It arrives on the doorstep in one way or another. Having refused it previously, it will nevertheless appear again as part of our path in life. Looking back, years later we might smile ruefully and see how much we squirmed and avoided what was a central truth of our lives.

The entire enterprise shifts when we see, think, feel, and surrender to our inner *yes*, our acceptance of the caregiving path before us. It will test us to the core, and the test will shape us into more of who we really are.

Recognition of this kind is a mystery. We can't argue with it, though we might try. It feels horrible, tremendous, scary, and yet so *right* in some unfathomable way. We can only proceed in the task by knowing that we have been in some way loved into it—remembered, revered, and recognized. It can then become for us holy work.

We don't really know what we have signed up for, do we? Somehow it just happened. Then every day is a school day in learning what care is. We also find out what care is not. Ever so slowly we become simplified, and re-created around caring. A new center emerges unbeknownst to us. We become part of the Mystery that is love.

I know this is mine to do.
I often wish that it were otherwise.
Your love has put me here.

If I avoid it,
I diminish myself.

If I take it on,
I must trust
that You will walk with me.

I wobble. I teeter.
But the truth is
that You have recognized me and therefore
I can recognize this love-task as mine.

I need Your help. Be by my side
Help me grow into the love
You trust me with.

Becoming Real

When the caregiving task is felt and known to belong to us, we take on the responsibility of it. It happens almost despite us. At the core an inner response, an inherent ability to respond, takes up the challenge that we will never know the full dimensions of. It's like finding oneself in midair before plunging into deep waters and beginning to swim.

Caregiving that arises through obligation, arm-twisting, or people pleasing is not true caregiving. It's a way to assuage doubt and to keep other people's expectations and criticisms from overwhelming us. There are many ego-based reasons to do what we are *not* called to do.

Under those auspices we will not have the deep resources of true response-ability. The caregiving that truly belongs to us is not only necessary for the person we are caring for, but also for us as well. It will make us whole in an inexplicable way.

All kinds of caregiving may look the same on the surface. Caregiving, as a profession for which one is paid, can be heartfelt. It may not seem on a par with voluntary caregiving in a family or for a friend, but at the core it is the quality of care that matters. Those who are getting the care can feel the difference. In one they are objectified. They are treated like a job to be done and gotten through. In the other they can sense themselves as persons who are valued. Person to person, response to response, such caregiving can feel like a gift from heaven. Even in the midst of pain, fatigue, and the seeming endlessness of the task, the gift of responding shines and sheds a light between giver and receiver.

Looking at response a little more deeply, we can see that it hinges on being present in the moment. Present, moment-to-moment, our lives become momentous. To live this way is to live a deep human capacity, one that requires something simple and very hard—willingness to pay attention beyond our own concerns. We have to be present to respond. Maybe we could say that it is only when we are present that we truly are persons. The rest of the time we are on an automatic program simply functioning and not really alive. We are in a kind of limbo.

The difference one feels when someone is truly present to us is a profound difference. It is a gift in which we are mutually made real.

How sad it is when I discover
how often the only world that matters to me
is the one I manufacture.

You are always here, and I am so often not here.
I see how much of my concerns are about me
and mine, and they distance me from Your love.

Bring me back.
Bring me into personhood again,
into deep response to You
and to others whom You love
and who are meant for me to love.

Let me not live an automatic life.
Help me to be present,
to use my heart and hands
in conscious care.

Egg on Our Faces

One of the biggest things we relinquish when we have recognized that we will be caregiving someone for the long haul is control. It is a stubborn, ongoing conundrum to have to take charge of what is needed in the care of another at the same time that we have to let go of the control of how things will turn out. It's like trying to drive with the brakes on and a broken GPS. To believe we can do this harmoniously is a total fantasy. We will struggle with it over and over again.

Letting go of control over how we want things to be done, or be, or even hope for, is to accept that we will be in misery and rattled a lot of the time. To enter into the paradox of taking charge and relinquishing control is to be willing to suffer, to be knocked off our pins. No matter how thoughtful, eloquent, or high-minded we want to be, we will end up with egg on our faces.

Then, why not begin each day with accepting egg on our faces to start with? We will find relief in giving up the hope of perfection and of certainty. Real life is messy as well as uncontrollable. It asks us to live as truthfully as we can and know that we are already in a sacred mess up to our armpits.

Mindfully washing our faces and hands can be a prayerful way to know egg has a place to be from time to time, and we will wash it away as best we can. To get things right for someone else is never going to be exactly right. We will mostly be in approximation, and that, by virtue of necessity, has to be good enough.

Relinquishing the false efforts that are buried in control will give us a ground of freedom, something real to stand on. Daily we will be doing our *toilette*, as the French put it. Our bodies naturally let go of what has been used and digested. We know that what has been ingested is no longer needed. In the same way we need to release the strain of a day of being in charge. We need to detox our minds and let go of expectations we have of ourselves. We do what we can and not what we can't.

Finding a corner of time and place to focus on relinquishing will help us to be clear. Letting go helps us to live more fully.

Here I am again thinking I know best
how things should be handled.
Isn't it me who knows
the best way, the smoothest way, the least costly way?

AAAH—look
at all the good ways I take charge!

Here I am caught again
in wanting to be good, relevant, capable,
and without blemish.

Help me to just do what is mine to do.
Help me feel that it is enough,
that I am enough.

Hold the reins for me.

Knowing We Don't Know

Respect for ourselves and for the one we care for is a central attitude to live and to be lived by. We simply do not, and will not, know the truth and fullness of anyone's personal life, for it is hidden even as we live it. Then to be respectful is first to give up thinking that we know what others are essentially about, and second, it is something we can hold on to, like a railing, while we learn as we go.

Who are we? Who is the one we care for? Who someone was at the vibrant age of twenty or later at the tottering age of eighty is still the same soul—a soul that has lived and learned, has suffered, made mistakes, and has loved and been loved. All that living can't be summed up as if one could add up a life like a column of numbers.

Things we have given of ourselves and set in motion are still unfolding somewhere in the vastness of what *is*. Both caregiver and care receiver are mysteries. Can we learn to respect that about each other and see that it makes for equality between us?

Because one person needs another, there can be a way we give and a way we receive that is diminishing. Suppose we can't do for ourselves. Suppose the one who is caring for us is burdened. Who is the needy one? Still, the one in charge has more control and more power. And deep down we know that power can corrupt. How easy it is to fall away from our basic equality, our basic, shared human neediness. How easily, in taking care of someone, we can lapse into an unconscious feeling of superiority and so act disrespectfully.

It's also true that a person needing care may lose all perspective about the needs of the one giving care. They might cajole, demand, and act more helpless than they are. Respect for the otherness of the other is missing. It is then imperative for caregivers to respect their own needs. When both sides of the equation go unattended, caregiving becomes a living hell. How important it is to know that having self-respect as a caregiver gives us the ability to give respect to the one we care for.

In the midst of bedpans, wheelchair transfers, and endless sitting by the bedside, we can nevertheless sense a tender and fragile blossom of respect opening a petal at a time. Respect is the growing medium that lets us become more of who we are. It is what lets us bloom even when we face death and disease. The meaning of our lives will never be summed up, but their beauty and fragrance can keep unfolding.

Daily I forget that I am Yours,
that You made me for love's sake,
that You hold my being with infinite respect.

May I receive that wondrous gift
and know it to be
a gift that's been given to everyone.
Let me cultivate respect
and extend it to those who are in the path of my life.

Let me not automatically think I know
what I am about or what others need.
Let my not knowing grow into being respectful.

CARE AND PRAYER

It Is What It is

With respect on our minds, we will surely find that we fall short of living it. We'll lose our tempers and feel sorry for ourselves, whether we are the ones being cared for or vice versa. We ask, *Why me? Why does life have to be this hard?*

Of course, there are no answers to these questions. Then, most likely, a deep sigh will come and perhaps a stoic numbness with words like *it is what it is*. Not comforting words at all, not what we want to hear. We plod along on the muddy road of our discontent having forgotten to respect our journey and its hidden gifts. How do we stop wallowing in the refrain of how unfair things are? How do we move on?

Let's take in the word *reframe*. It does not ask us to be different than we are. Right this minute we may be disrespectful, and it doesn't feel good. We know an artist can put different frames on the very same picture. Each time the work of art is reframed it takes on a different cast. Could we take what is happening and put a different frame around it?

Suppose we experimented with making our frame dark and full of nicks and deep gouges? With such a frame we'd see our circumstances in an even more despairing way. Then if we changed the frame to one with buttercups and butterflies, we'd see a different take on our situation, but it would probably not be one we could say was truthful.

Having experimented with reframing, we might see that we can dwell in possibility as well as in exaggerated negativity. *Sleep on it*, the wise saying goes. Much hopelessness comes with fatigue. Even a little nap can open doors letting in more ways of looking at things. We may perk up just a little. It's still *the same old, same old*, but now we can perhaps put a different frame on things, or we can trust Spirit to do the framing. We can step away, then, as artists of our lives and see the picture from a more gracious distance. It will feel to be more than just *what it is*.

Problems are never solved from the consciousness in which they were created. By surrendering the framing job, we do not make our situation worse or better. We already know that being able to witness without assessment is a profound grace. Then the saying, *it is what it is*, will no longer feel like a prison sentence but an opportunity to go on with a little more objectivity. Our situation is not who we are. That dis-identification helps us claim ourselves apart from what is occurring. It allows us to know that we always live within God's framework.

Please give me different eyes
to see where I am.
I'm clouded with fatigue
and full of feeling sorry for myself
and for the ones I care for.

I know pity is not compassion.
It's sentimental.
Teach me love instead.

Let me not forget that even if
any of us makes our beds in hell,
You are there.

Give me a better frame of mind.
Let me know Your love holds me,
and that everything
is in Your keeping.

Tumbled to the Shore

A stone in the ocean is tumbled to shore, pulled back into the sea and tumbled to the shore again. Little by little it is smoothed and rounded. It also grows smaller and more refined. It will in time, perhaps many years from now, become sand. Perhaps it will further dissolve into the elements it is composed of. It will go back to where it came from.

Our work as caregivers will tumble us and refine us. Our edges will hopefully be worn away, and like sea-tumbled stones that are good to hold, we may in time find that we can do the work in a smoother way and that our care receivers will want to hold our hands.

For sure, we will always encounter the unexpected, the storms that toss us around. They will come. They will surely come! How do we live their impact on us? Perhaps the first thing to notice is that they are not personal, out to get us, even though they affect us. They just *are*.

Taking things personally is actually a form of pride, an attitude that assumes we are special and should be treated as such. After all, with a special status nothing adverse should come to us, right? But taking things personally can also be a form of self-deprecation. Of course, this would happen to me because deep down I'm not good enough. I don't count. I have to expect things to go wrong for me.

Caregiving is a refining process. It will bring out the unconscious and often hidden convictions we have in us— the good and not so good. It's just human nature to want to look good to ourselves and leave the rest forgotten. But we will be awakened many nights by the truth.

Stephen Levine, the great teacher about death and dying, used to say that knowing ourselves was one insult after the other. But let's change that to be one acceptance after the other. We will align with the refining process when we orient that way. We'll not have to feel that we are victims of circumstance. We can instead take up being participators in life as it is.

Haven't we seen this instinct when a tragedy has occurred in our communities? People feel it strongly and pitch in. We become part of what is happening. We lose our separating tendencies and dive into the human experience that is happening now. We somehow can't help but help. This is about *us* and not just about *me*. In that shift our essence is revealed as refined and full of dignity.

Day after day life tumbles me,
knocks me around
and caresses me.
I lose parts of me that I thought were me.

This is hard but it is gentle also.
It is a paradox I do not understand.

Help me be accepting.
Let me be rounded into wholeness
and in time, dissolved as sea-stones
are dissolved becoming sand
and returning to the place they came from.

Whether I am controlling, and jagged,
self-determined and willfully separated
from You,
or growing smooth despite myself,
let me be Yours to refine.

Those Kin to Us

To do what has to be done day after day is to be present without the illusion that things will get easier. Perhaps some days are a little easier, but sooner or later the difficult ones show up. It is those days that blow out the inner flame and leave us in a wallow of darkness. This can probably never be skipped as an experience. It happens on both sides of the caregiving equation—the caregiver and the care receiver.

That depth of difficulty cannot be denied and should not be denied. It is a state where naked helplessness resides, and it is a state that is profoundly human. Some mystics live there all the time without light for decades. They live in unknowing love. Some people in deep depression know it well. In the word kindred is the word *kin*. *Kin* is also in kindness, as well as the word kindle. To sense, even a little, those who are kin to us in those dark states can be of huge help. Their presence helps us feel less alone, for they are not strangers to keeping going despite the absence of light.

Being there is a kind of creature-sensing—a breathing side by side, without lights, plans, and without fixing anything. It is a shared vulnerability, a profound intimacy that warms us just enough to help us continue. Often in such wordless sharing something strikes us like a match on a rough surface, A little flame appears. We are rekindled. The light becomes for us a witness to the situation we are in. We see anew with more kinship. Often this gives us courage enough to take the next step we need to take. The whole journey to the end can be taken with these small, illuminated steps.

Rekindling can't be forced. We know it is a gift. For it to happen, however, is to know there is both a wick and fuel inside us that are not our own but given to us as a birthright. Allowing ourselves to be in the dark is a prayer of trust and a knowing that things are not ultimately up to us. It is in the dark times that we are stopped in our striving and insistence that things should be other than they are.

We often don't know what we really need and go after things in a compensatory way, a way that just keeps taking us into more of the same. We need to learn that the limits of *what can be* may turn out to be a gift. We need to lean into what is present even though it's hard. Perhaps, only then, a light is given to us, a light that we do not produce, but a light that is revealed as gift. That light is hard to blow out. It isn't ours, but it is ours to see by, and it will rekindle us.

For me to think I can do this caregiving
out of my own resources
is a way to be quickly wrapped in darkness.
All lights out.

Then I'll have no wick or flame.
I'll have darkness.

May grace be near me.
May those others who understand
and share this experience come close,
their fears mingled with mine.

Together in human kinship
Your Presence will find us.
We'll have a chance to be rekindled
with a lasting flame.

Treading Water

Rekindled, and given another day to live, we need aware-
ness to remove attitudes and habits that take away our inner
light. This self-knowing is hard work. So much of what leads
us into stymied places is automatic in us. We have a *poor me*
tape, or an *I'm not enough* tape, or an *it's not fair* tape. These
tapes seem to have a life of their own. When we pay close
enough attention, we'll hear them whir and loop through
our days. To have them go away, these hidden convictions
can't just be recognized. That's simply a first step. They
also need to be dismantled, a tall order especially if they
have been around a long time. There is a tarry, smoky satisfaction about being the first to put our selves down. Then,
when others do, we are prepared for the worst because it

has already happened. We've shielded ourselves by thinking we know before anyone else how right we are about what is wrong with us. That way, we remain in control.

Those tapes won't be dissolved in an instant. The power they have had over us needs to be replaced by something else, something we long for more than being confident about having control. The security we feel in our old convictions seems to be a buoy in heavy seas. At least what we've always felt to be true is happening as waves overwhelm us. It gives us some kind of explanation of why things are the way they are. We may have unconsciously made these tapes when we were very young having little life experience and probably not enough support.

To feel we are at sea when we are caregiving is very common. That's when we reach for those old convictions. What would it take to allow our negative tapes to be replaced? There is really not much time while caregiving to notice that we are caught in negative self-assessment. But the need for a different inner story can show up when we wake in the middle of the night in a sweat, or when one more unexpected thing gets piled on the pile that is already too much. We have no choice but to let go, and that is the faltering beginning of grace.

Most of us can't remove the tapes entirely, but we can move them away a little. It takes courage to speak up and say to the nagging inner voice, *You are absolutely right, but just now I don't need to be right. Please be quiet now. Besides, you know there may be other things that are also right. Let me see if I can tread water without you.* Even just one such successful lived moment will bring us closer to shore. Treading water allows for time, for grace, and for new ways to think.

I'm at sea again.
Too many tasks swamp me.
I can't keep up.

Those old feelings of not being enough
cascade over me.
I feel I am drowning.

Wave upon wave.
I can't catch my breath.
I am so scared, and I have to let go.

Replace my self-reliance with Your Presence.
Be my buoy.
Let me trust
that You will not let me face these perils alone.

Mutual Compassion

Stressed to the max, bound by relentless routine, or simply bored, we erupt in ways that are not gracious. We bark in frustration or with a startling, though momentary, meanness. When the storm has passed, we'll face how we behaved.

Guilt is useless. In guilt we simply make ourselves feel bad, and usually there is also a hidden feeling of being justified in our outrage. Most likely, under the same pressure, something within us will repeat what we don't want to do, and we'll feel guilty again.

Remorse is another thing entirely. In the spirit of remorse, we accept and know we are unable to be in control. We don't hide in self-justifications. We truly feel what we have done and face ourselves in all our faults. Remorse allows us to be truthful with ourselves and with the person we hurt. We are not asking them for forgiveness. We are owning the whole, sorry story. Bishop Tutu's great healing work in South Africa hinged on *truth and reconciliation*. Without truth there cannot be reconciliation.

Barking at our patient, mother, father, or child is not heinous, but we know in their disease and need that they are more helpless than we are. We have the advantage of being in a position, at least just for now, to be a little more physically healthy or capable than they are.

It's only human, we might say in excuse. That, too, is the truth. But the deeper truth is that we let fly and took it out on someone in our care with less strength and fewer resources. We abandoned the field of mutual compassion. How then do we return to care? Mutual compassion is seeing the bigger picture of how things arose. Nothing is our entire fault. Nothing is the care receiver's entire fault. The bigger picture includes countless demands, too little time for self-care, unrealistic expectations of ourselves, unrealistic expectations of those who need care or those who assign us to care for their loved ones.

There is also a convergence, a history that brought our situation into being. Remorse must include the whole truth. Dividing the world into good and bad, black and white, your fault only or my fault only, is not the truth. We are always in mutuality even when things are happening that we feel badly about.

I did it again.
I lost it.
What I don't want to do, I do.

Cradle me, Lord.
Remorse is so heavy.
Help me stop taking things on
that are too much for me.

Only You see the whole picture.
Help me lean into the courtesy of Your love
that knows all our frailties
and loves us nonetheless.

Let receiving Your healing love be
what I pass on to those for whom I care.

On Different Rails

Being remorseful over and over again is spiritually harmful. It is a lack of trust. If our remorse comes out of a deep, true place, then release is the natural outcome. We are no longer defining ourselves by the mistakes or regrets we have, but on allowing and trusting that our journey can continue.

There used to be *linemen* in old railroad times. A juncture in the rails would need to be changed so a train could take a different path along rails that led in a different direction. When remorse is deep and true, the train of events stops for a little time in order for our tracks to be shifted. That little time is a holy moment. Something is being laid down for us, and we are no longer living in the past. We are not in the future either, but in a moment of profound trust. We let what was be as it was. Perhaps we are able to feel how the inner coupling for a new direction and way to live happens by grace. How strange that not fighting the truth helps us move on.

Releasing can be a daily practice, and not just for surrendering the mistakes of the past. Just as we can't inhale a new breath before exhaling an old one, we need to release the events of our daily lives into God's keeping. We can allow times for recoupling. Those times do not need to be long. They are more like *breath breaks* to let the brakeman or woman in us be sure we are going where we really mean to go. Release always seems to bring us more energy and a lighter feeling.

Release, then, is ongoing and deeper than these small pauses that keep us from derailing. It is a sturdy trust that God loves our littleness—our weaknesses, our very humanness—and can use all that has been to unfold in the direction of more life and love. Our destination is God, and our journey is in God as well. Our part is to stay in faithful connection to the guidance that is there when we stop and listen and consciously let go of as much as we can. We need to breathe deeply to have a new lease on life. Those breath-taking moments are times we can sense much more what is meant for us to do, and what we are to leave alone.

Sometimes I don't feel that it's safe to let things go.
I know that faith in You is what will help me.
Teach me that release is natural and necessary.
Help me to let things just be
every single day.

CARE AND PRAYER

Help me know
that all is in Your keeping, even my mistakes.
Let my remorse about them be released also.
Let my life's direction and my destination be You.
In You, all is made new
Every moment is a journey
in You and to You.

The Boomerang of Love

Whenever we are doing things out of habit, obligation, or to look good to others whom we want to impress, we are enslaved. We get fed up easily and grow resentful. It is important to come to an understanding of what is ours to do that is not merely obligation but something heartfelt and true. When we know what that is, we have found a connection to freedom and inner joy.

How we relate to the calling of care is a deep subject. When we are devoted to the task, energy comes to us that helps us be constant in the work of caring as well as in overcoming the obstacles that always show up in the process. Let's keep in mind that those we care for are *not* extensions of us. They are sacred *others* who need to grow even as they are recovering or while they are diminishing. Their growth is not our responsibility. It belongs to them. Deep healing may be won and yet not show up as a physical cure. We know that to care is to offer a non-invasive relatedness that will almost always be felt as love because we are not imposing an outcome. We are being available to what appears as necessary to handle at any given time and allowing for the mystery of inner healing to take place.

When we are living in the caregiving that furthers another's spirit and growth, we will grow as well, even in the midst of the difficulties that will surely arise. Furtherance for the growth and spirit of the other may not be visible to folks who witness us in our task. But Spirit will notice. A deeper resource than our own is present.

We will feel our place in the world when we live what it is we want to do wedded to what we feel we must do. That combination is always a high adventure even if it may seem dogged and boring to others.

Devoted to the sacred growth of the one we are caring for, we are living love. And most of us know that devoted love is a boomerang. When we give our love freely, love comes zipping back to embrace us.

This must not in any way be confused with parasitic dependence. We are each sacred beings in our own skins, and our lives are meant to enhance those we live with, and also enhance those creative ideas and commitments we have that express our personal goals.

When we relate in care with our entire person, we will feel confirmed by life itself. We will also confirm the worth of the one whose care is in our keeping. Is there anything that can be more tender to do in this world?

I need to claim what I sense and feel
I truly want to do.

With Your help, let it also be wedded to
what I must do.

Then,
a full purpose will emerge for me
and will be of deep meaning.

As I relate to the one I care for, I will know
that my own journey and theirs
will be journeys of growth
and through them
we will confirm one another.

Our journeys are linked.
We arrive together
though sometimes not at the same time.

We can trust
that love knows the way
even though we might not have a sense
of how and where to go.

The Right to *Be*

On either side of caregiving, tensions can arise that take us to a hard edge. We snap, hurting ourselves in the process, and maybe hurting the one we care for too. Many caregivers become so depleted that they lose a sense of their own worth. In the process they may also lose a sense of the worth of the person they are caring for. Every day becomes a day to *get through*. Personhood is forgotten, and only the *job and functioning* remain. The giving of care has taken everything. It sets the stage for subtle abuse.

How do we refuse abuse? At all times we need to remember that whatever happens is not one person's fault. So many factors are at play. For the caregiver, those factors can be too little rest, perhaps minimal resources, no time for self-expression, no time off, no help from others, and no appreciation.

For the one being cared for, some things that might be at play are the sense of life slipping away, feeling no longer wanted or needed, experiencing too much physical pain, or that they are a burden to others. But someone else might be demanding. The patient isn't patient but feels owed. They feel they can say anything they want without regard for the feelings of others. They can even be physically abusive, striking out in frustration and despair.

Because the scales are so uneven, it will most likely be the caregiver who has to handle the situation. Abuse escalates if it is not stopped. It must be refused. Perhaps the most important thing a caregiver can do when they are being abused is to walk into another room and give themselves space as long as their charge is relatively safe. It never works to argue with abuse. Caregivers must have enough self-regard to not be a target even when their empathy understands why it is happening. If things have come to this pass, the caregivers must have a place to lay their heads, to speak truthfully about what is occurring.

We understand that someone feeling cornered will either give up and crumple or lash out. Cornered by too many tasks, too little time, and too little help, not enough breathing room or self-expression, how can a meaningful life be lived? Taking responsibility for their own care as caregivers is to refuse the abuse of overwork. It is essential to befriend the right to *be* as much as the dedication to do.

When the walls shrink, when I find myself snapping,
help me refuse abuse.

When I am asked for too much,
when the person I care for behaves meanly,
let me step away.
Let me not be cornered.

Help me remember my worth
as Your beloved child.

Help me find new ways to work
with the shared frustration
my charge and I have.

Give us both breathing room.
Uphold us in Your grace.

Just Us Here Now

We will always keep growing, and we don't have to be more than we are. The caregiving enterprise is taxing, so learning to relax is one of the most valuable things we can do for ourselves and for the ones we care about.

Before our bodies can relax, our minds have to relax. To practice dropping responsibilities for a little while, and more importantly, dropping the roles we have taken on, is crucial. A *just-me-here-now* time every day can keep us from burnout. Looking deeply into the give and take of caregiving, we'll know on a gut level that we are just human, basically not different from one another despite the circumstances we are in. We want and need the same things—safety, companionship, appreciation, mutual care, and to have the basic needs of our bodies met.

Seeing how vulnerable we are, and actually all of us are, levels the field. Yes, some of us have more friends and apparent help. Some of us have more financial resources, but in the end we'll all have to drop false efforts to be with what is actually happening in our lives. We'll discover over and over again that we can only be ourselves and do what we can with what is at hand.

Paradoxically, learning to acknowledge our common needs lets us go about things in a more leisurely way. This is hard to describe. But anyone who has successfully dropped their role and entered the sanctity of mutuality will not only find relaxation but also find energy.

Practicing many little moments of *just-us-here-now* will surprise us with their power and depth. We'll experience a bit of internal spaciousness. The surprise is that we get more of who we are. To gently and simply relax with the person we are caring for will help them relax as well. We will find ourselves in the sweet mystery of being together in simply *being*. It will bring us closer. It will affirm the preciousness of each in the care equation. We will have managed to drop our differences for a moment and find our basic human goodness again.

The body is always reacting behind the mind. When we can relax our thinking, the tension in our bodies will shift also. But the body needs time to catch up with the mind, and when it does, an opening to soulfulness is possible. We can't force relaxation any more than we can force anything without causing resistance. We can be open to it, however, and maybe we could rename it free-laxation?

Called to this giving of care
let me not tense up like a taut wire.
Let me drop my roles.

Instead, help me to recognize
that we are here together,
not to fix anything, but to experience
together the love-current
that is You in us,
which runs in us both.

Let loving breaths fill my lungs.

Let us breathe together
relaxing into Your love and presence.

The Help of Others

Burnout dogs the heels of caregivers sometimes without their realizing what is happening to them until they are completely flattened. We can sense that it may be happening when we are frequently frustrated and perhaps treating our charge with less than common courtesy. We might even find a subtle tone of hauteur in our communication. Then it is high time to call for HELP. We have to give up any ideals of self-reliance that we might cherish. There is no such thing. All of us will always need the help of others.

A request is different from a demand. A true request has humility at its core. We surrender to knowing that we cannot do what needs doing alone any longer. We own our vulnerability without excusing it, and caring for it instead. Courtesy is needed when we approach those from whom we are requesting help, knowing they are vulnerable also and may need to turn us down because of what is on their plates.

A request needs to be specific and have time limits. To ask for someone to shop for us, for instance, or to stay with our charge while we shop for food, is specific and time limited. We are not asking for the moon. We are requesting a little needed time. When requests have such boundaries they are less likely to be turned down. They are *one-time* requests. However, they give the person whom we ask a chance to see the bigger picture of where they find us, and often that leads to offers of future help.

We should never underestimate what our appreciation of help gives back to another. Many studies have been made about what satisfaction in the workplace consists of. A decent salary, of course, but much more important is being appreciated. It promotes loyalty, and sometime workers will even take less in pay because they know how much they are valued.

When our requests are not laced with a demanding tone, we open up a channel of mutual giving and appreciation. *I need you and I feel a great deal of appreciation for your help* becomes wedded to *I am happy to help and feel honored to do so.* Here, then, is human graciousness. We are living interdependence—a truthful human state that is neither independence nor dependence.

Learning to make requests specific and time limited while showing our deep appreciation will keep us out of isolation and place us into relationships and communities of care. We are not in this task alone.

Sometimes I feel
I cannot ask for help.
I feel diminished by needing it.

Help me to allow
the truth of my vulnerability.
Let me not be ashamed of my limitations.

Let me allow care for me
while caring for another.

How amazing is an open receiving hand
when met by an open giving hand.
We confirm one another
beyond circumstance.

We are meeting in an exchange
far bigger than either of us.
Together we are in this
not solely for our own sakes
but for Love's sake.

Love's Hands and Feet

On reflection, response is different from responsibility. We cannot help but respond to what is happening around us and in us. But that will not necessarily make us responsible or devoted to someone or something. There are so many stimuli that if we were to respond to all of them, we would go crazy. Our minds shut things off that are sensed to be peripheral to us. We need that self-preservation in order to live.

What is ours to do? How do we know? It is intrinsic in human nature to be drawn to care for others or for ideals and issues that matter. What is ours to respond to with devotion and steadfastness may not be the caring we are asked to take up just because a need presents itself in our families or in our communities. If we go ahead anyway and offer our help, we will not feel that the caring we do completes us. It will be make-work. Real caregiving needs to be more central to us so that we can act with fullness of heart. If it is truly central, then we will accept the suffering that goes with showing up for the one we care about. It will not be a short-term thing. It will be a place we grow into, a place of becoming.

Suppose we were musicians. Then, we would practice endless scales in order to serve the music. If we are called to caregiving, we accept the ups and downs, the losses, the fatigue, and the confinement. We will also discover a tenderness that wells up as we do what we do. We will be opened. Not only will we experience that we are capable of love, but that mysteriously we have become a dwelling place for Love itself. This turns everything upside down. It is then Love that loves, and we are its hands and feet.

Reflection of this kind is not a mental thing. We can't think it or imagine it, to have it be so. We can't even really know it except as a wind is known in a gale. We experience wind by being buffeted by a storm, or we feel it caress us in a soft, summer breeze. This mystery will not happen to us if caring for another is only happenstance or a stopgap thing.

That is how things should be, for there must be other ways to respond in the world where our gifts can unfold and be needed. We can be engaged in another meaning that belongs to us. *Let what we love be what we do,* said Rumi. To respond is automatic, but to respond because something is loved from the core and takes us beyond our usual comforts is an entirely different thing. When we respond from a depth of love our gifts will be freely given. They will complete us.

I know I need to use my gifts
for my life to find its meaning.

Help me to reflect on where and how
to give of myself.
Let me help, but let me not be cornered
into false giving for false reasons:
not being able to say "no," saying "yes" to please.
Let me hear my own deep yearnings.

Let the love
You have planted within me
inform how I respond.

Help me discern what is mine to do
in Love's name.

The Art of Living

To ask for help implies receiving, doesn't it? People can give us things or their emotional support, but if we don't receive what is given, the gifts will be meaningless to us. It is also true that we can't fully *do* caring unless we *are* caring. To *be* care is not something we accomplish on our own. It is something we are given not just once, but over and over again. We don't own it. We serve the gift of it. We become care in the day-to-day doing of it. The love and care with which we are able to love and care is a gift from God. It is not a one-time gift. It is a process gift meant to be developed and embodied. We need to receive that gift and to lend ourselves to its unfolding.

There is then, to various degrees in us all, a need to care, be it for another human being, a cause, or an idea. We need that *other* to become more fully ourselves. When we step back from the daily tasks of care, we can notice that it is the central current running through all our tasks. It makes us care-full. It's not so hard to consider being willing servants, not so much of the person we are caring for but to the gift of care inside us. *Since love grows within you, so beauty grows. For love is the beauty of the soul*, said Augustine of Hippo. Let's be artists of life, then, working with what we have and where we are. We'll know we are not caring simply because it is a necessity. We are caring because something given to us asks us to give of ourselves. We feel the tug of becoming care from deep inside. It is the beauty of our souls.

This may seem philosophically useless in the midst of medicine bottles and wheelchair transfers. But deeply felt, we can be infused with courage to continue at times when the going is rough, when we are tired and hopeless. No ounce of care is ever lost in the universe. As Julian of Norwich put it, *The smallest thing will not be forgotten.* The ones we care for may not be cured, but they can be valued, given love, and respect. And we, as caregivers, are confirmed by our commitment and constancy. Even in exhaustion and the certainty of future loss, we can find that being present as best we can, with what we have and where we are, has worth and beauty. It creates something palpable though perhaps not easily visible.

Holding the hand of our charge we are partners in a process. We are growing—perhaps into death and into the depths of loss, but also into the love-truth of mutual value. We are together in God's care—small and vulnerable, courageous and scared, gentle and strong, confused and certain, and of infinite beauty. We are the art of living.

> *In the profusion of all that has to be done,*
> *which seems to be all of the time,*
> *I know a current of care upholds me*
> *and enfolds me.*
> *It is Your care living in me.*

May I receive it.

When nothing seems to go right,
when there are not enough resources
You draw me into the unknown.

You draw me to the edge where love waits
side by side with despair,
where suffering brings growth and surrender,
where Your Presence is a constant.

Even though it is difficult, let me accept
the need to be about care,
no matter how difficult.

Keep me constant
so that Your love will flow through me.

Suffering Side by Side

When caregiving of another person goes on a long time, it can feel like a desert experience. The ground is strewn with stony obstacles. It's dry and seemingly lifeless. It may be of help for those in contemplative faith traditions to remember that in ancient times those seeking God chose to live in the desert to do their inner work of faith.

We may not have deliberately signed up to take care of someone. We may have just found ourselves in the job. If it continues without letup, we enter a dimension of living that might be likened to the experience of the desert mothers and fathers of the past. They were taught by the hardships of desert living. It was a school of intense self-discovery. Those gutsy souls were instructed to learn everything they needed to know by remaining faithful in their cells. All around them the spare, bleak desert extended as far as their eyes could see.

This turns out to be the school of surrender. It teaches us to remain connected to what *is*, no matter how difficult. It develops stability, a signature trait of faith. This is not about having warm, fuzzy feelings for those we care for. It is not about being heroic, either. In desert experiences we have to pay close attention to exactly what is happening and not deviate into self-pity or empathic gooeyness. It is rather a deep honoring of that which is ours to integrate. The list can be long: our negativity, our regrets, our limits, our forsaken hopes and possibilities, our triumphs and moments of splendor.

There is endless time and space in the desert, but not for wallowing. It is a place for clear perceiving, for presence and conscious devotion. Deeper than devotion to the person we are caring for is the devotion to Spirit, who gives us the strength to endure for the sake of our soul work.

As much as we need to take up our inner stories, we must also let our charges take up theirs if they are conscious enough to do so. What a person approaching death or severe limitation must come to terms with *is* their work. We must not take it away from them with mistaken *helpfulness*. Conscious suffering is a path of enormous spiritual power.

Then, suffering side by side can be understood as a shared desert experience that is able to open doors in us that our egos could never open. It can bring us to deep experiences of grace. Are we up to being in such an arid, sun-scorched terrain? Not by our own will. We are led there. With God's presence and our willingness to remain in the heat of self-discovery, we will enter the mystery of becoming God's own. We will become sanctuaries of care.

Day after day I am here
at the stony edge
of wanting to run away.

Day after day I am being taught stability,
not by any heroic measures but by living close
to the ground with the stones I trip over,
stones I am to clear and move away.

Only day by day, remaining in this cell
of care do I have a chance to find my true self,
and love's claim on me and my care partner.

We will discover again and again
that we are Yours,
that You never leave us to face
what we must face alone.

With-dom

We shall never regret having cared for somebody. It will be a cornerstone in our lives. We may regret not having cared enough or having had lapses in our caring. But being *for* someone else to support their being and unfolding is a confirmation of the preciousness of life itself. Our being and meaning is revealed in our capacity to set ourselves aside, not by ignoring our needs, but by focusing with love and interest on the life and needs of another.

We've already established that regretting our mistakes should be short-lived. We are to notice them, yes. And we are to learn from them. More important, we are to move on, to embrace being *with* the one we care for to the best of our abilities. Would we regret learning what matters to our charges? No.

Would we regret communicating that we understand those we care for more and more as time goes on? No. Would we regret making them comfortable? No. Every small attempt to walk in another's shoes will open us to more of reality. It will help us take more appropriate action for their benefit.

We do not have to live for another at the exclusion of our own lives. That would be regrettable. But we can live in the spirit of companionship. We can be *with* someone and *for* someone and not lose ourselves. We can help them find ways to be more comfortable and to live with more meaning. A person who has a caregiver who seeks to understand and support them, who lets them be as they are in their process of healing or dying, will be deeply treasured. Those caregivers have a deep wisdom. It's really *with-dom*, isn't it?

As caregivers we will make many mistakes. We won't, and perhaps can't, do the job perfectly. It's too big and too constant. But if, under all the ups and downs, we have not lost the heart of being *with* another, our efforts will be good enough.

Regrets are not meant to burden us. A true regret is an uncomfortable blessing but a needed one. Remorse and regret are different though they are close cousins. True remorse is a change agent. Regret has more to do with acceptance of our choices and not wishing for another past. Could we on a regular basis look back on a week of caregiving and notice where we feel we could have done a little better? Could we do this without being puritanical? We would then be with ourselves as well as with the one in our keeping.

Caregiving is messy, tiring, and immensely meaningful. It allows us to grow and to know ourselves more and more as we give ourselves away.

It is my intent to let this day be a day of being
"for" the one I care about.

Let me not forget this and then regret it.

That does not mean that I will
mechanically do whatever is asked of me.
I would soon regret not having
kept good boundaries.

Let my heart lead me in all I do today.
It is my heart that is able to be
side by side with suffering.

It is my heart that has "with-dom."
May I live in the circle of its embrace.

Claiming Our Intentions

We know caregiving is poignant, transformative, exhausting, relentless, and deeply meaningful. For some of us it is a choice-less choice. Caregivers seem to be born to the task and roll up their sleeves for another day of caregiving doing what needs to be done. Others linger on the threshold with an unspoken *Do I have to?* or *I can't do it!* They come to caregiving reluctantly and rise to the occasion as best they can while struggling with the consuming task it is.

But either way could we imagine a world without the kind efforts of others? It would soon be a hell.

Looking more deeply into how intentions make our caregiving a conscious choice can help. We know having choices is central to having a meaningful life. Without examining our intentions and our choices we have no freedom. We need to claim as much as possible what we do with our days even though those days inherently have limits.

How different a day of caregiving would be to us if we claimed it as a way to be true to a larger commitment, a commitment to our values, our promises to others, and our willingness to be about love. Sipping our morning coffee or tea, we could quietly begin the day by sipping in the warmth and depth of our dedication and devotion.

Knowing something belongs to us to do gives us strength. Quietly claiming and reclaiming our commitments is like refueling. We know that we know where we belong, and what the very next steps might be that we should take. There's no way to see the whole of the caregiving journey. But we have the day before us, and our hearts need to be in our doing. We need to daily confirm our intentions.

In the process of claiming and reclaiming, we may find that some aspect of the caregiving we have been doing is no longer right for us to do. We need to stop or change course or include caregiving for our needs as well. For the sake of the one we are caring for, if our heart is not in the task, we must bow out. There is nothing more awful on the receiving end of care than to be treated by a person with absence of heart.

We can also be on automatic pilot, helping, helping, and helping as a way to avoid an inner ache of our own. In that kind of arrangement lies a depth of old sorrow that needs tending. Taking the time to understand may help us to get care for those forgotten places inside us. It is not unusual that people who have been neglected as youngsters turn to caregiving as their work in life.

Here's another day to be aware,
to do simple things
that help another person live.

This could easily be me needing help.
How vulnerable we all are.
Let me not lose heart
but gain heart-fullness.

Help me to know if I am giving care
as an expression of myself
or as a way to avoid myself.

Let me daily reclaim
what is truly mine to do.

Ordering Our Days

Caring has a way of ordering our days and our priorities. It doesn't so much impose something rigid on us from the outside as make us choose what is the best for the one we care for. What is irrelevant has to be dropped. Sometimes that may be costly, but we do it because our path of caring is central to us.

There will be things we once wanted to be about that are now a hindrance to us. We structure our days to make a better schedule. We pay attention to what we cook and serve when diet turns out to be of importance. We rearrange our homes to make for easier movements if our charges are in walkers or wheelchairs. We may even move to a new place that will make caregiving simpler.

Caring orders us inwardly too. We may study and learn about illnesses and how best to handle them. We may attend lectures, write letters, and seek counsel to feel more helpful and informed for our care partners. Our worlds will open to others who are in the same boat. We may join support groups to enhance the lives we are living.

We will also be drawn to others who are caregivers because their presence supports us, and because we share a mutual interest. Being in the task together reinforces us and gives us the opportunity for mutual support.

People who give themselves to others have a quality of being that we are inevitably drawn to.

All of these changes do not have to be thought of as enslavements. They are ways to grow in our task of embodying love and care. We give up some things for things that have more value to us. This reinforces the sacredness of caregiving. We come to a deep sense of purpose and fulfillment even though the task asks us for a lot.

Olympic athletes, for instance, will order their lives to become better at their sport. They will eat to support their bodies, sleep to recover from massive physical efforts, and live fully for their commitment. It isn't easy, and it is meaningful. They accept what it takes to do what they are committed to do. Their commitment gives them a place where they belong. Caregiving can give us that validation. It reinforces where we belong and how we belong. That can mean we are set apart because of the needs of our charges. We may not then be in the mainstream any longer, but we'll be in the love-stream. The extent we are involved with the giving of care is something no one can decide for us. It may simply be peripheral or it may take most of our time. There is no life that is not made more meaningful through the gift of caregiving. The task orders our lives, reinforces our values, and places us where we sense we belong.

If caregiving
has somehow chosen me, I am not submitting.
I'm surrendering—opening
to the invitation to be
more inclusive, more engaged, more me.

I surrender to
what I feel belongs to me,
however difficult.

I can be made whole even in suffering.
The gift of caring takes me beyond myself
to the raw beauty of love and its costs.

It reinforces that I am in the right place
where I open further and live in grace.

Refuge

As caregivers we know that repeated complaints about *all the awful things we have to do and be* can keep us in a dark place. Done in the earshot of the one we are caring for, it really is a shot. It injures. Our unthinking words will complicate what is already complicated. No one wants to feel they are a burden to another. No one who has immense limitations, and is already helpless, wants to hear how they are badly impacting another person's life when they can't do anything about it. Great care and custody of our words are central to caregiving.

But central for us is also being seen and understood. Someone's tender and listening support can be a refuge. We usually think of a refuge as being a safe location set apart where we will not be harmed. But why couldn't a relationship in which we are lovingly heard be considered a refuge? We need someone from time to time to hear us out. We are not dumping then, but sharing our truth as we see it. That is different from constant complaint.

To ask for someone's loving ear takes courage. This can be a friend, a colleague, or a professional counselor. To be someone's ear is also courageous. On both sides of the coin there need to be boundaries. A refuge is not a refuge without them. We set aside land for wildlife. The places have parameters, so many acres of fields, forests, or wetlands. So, too, we need to set aside time and space for the sharing and hearing process. It needs to be safe. It needs to be contained. The internal wildness we each have needs a place to burrow, romp, cry, and fly. Can we listen with acceptance and allow someone to have whatever it is they need to feel for a time? Can we be spacious letting them bark, weep, howl, and sing? Can we be a safe refuge for another? Can another be a refuge for us?

Nestled in the word *hear* is the word *ear*. We have eyelids, but we don't have ear-lids. That is probably because in the early times of our evolution it was important to hear if something hostile was approaching. It was a matter of life and death for early humans so they could be ready to defend themselves. Now we need empathic listening more than strategic hearing. We need loving ears so we can blow off steam and not worry that we are hurting the one we care for.

Being able to listen that way is not to be bound up in another person's trouble. It is the clean task of witnessing and of holding a safe space for them. It is to keep a steady horizon in mind, knowing that things will pass, that time will heal, and that loving is an enormous landscape with lush fields and deep, scary crags. All of us will need such a refuge from time to time.

I need space and a loving ear.
I need to be heard so I can
better listen to the one I care for.

I need refuge, a place to be safe
for just a short time. I am so crowded
inside with things unspoken,
and with things I long for.

I need to snarl, to tell someone
who will understand that there are days
I want to bark and bite.

I need refuge
for the animal need in me
for space, air, and time.
I need someone's caring and spacious ear.

I know to be understood feels like sanctuary.
May I do this for someone in their need.
May I ask for it in my need.
May we take refuge in one another.

Off the Books

When we reconcile our checkbooks we can see what we have in our accounts and what we have spent. We usually try to get it down to the penny. We're probably also thinking about those deposits that need to be made for future expenditures.

When we try to reconcile emotional and physical expenditures, we know quite a bit by feeling it, but we'll sense even more that we don't really know.

We can guess about the future, but it is the present that will teach us that we'll never see the whole picture. Probably a very good thing! We will have to accept being in partial darkness. The ground we think we stand on is constantly moving and shifting. Living without certitude is the truth of the human condition. We need to be reconciled to impermanence, change, and the tender vulnerability that is at the core of life.

We can't keep accounts on this, but we can learn by experience and by living consciously. We are always in the semi-darkness of paradox. How curious that spending our-selves in devoted ways expresses our whole selves and fills us.

More of a paradox is that a difficult challenge will help us grow, and so it may become a large asset. There's no way logic can reconcile these things. How astounding, then, that being constant eventually liberates us. Daily we reconcile what we have to do with what we want to do. The columns won't make sense. Giving up on hard facts may help us settle into knowing that just showing up is a living prayer. Somehow a revolving credit of goodness is under everything.

We didn't earn it, but in prayer we have access to it.

To reconcile is to match up thoughts, work, feelings, challenges, and good and bad surprises, with uncertainty, trust, partial knowing, personal grit, and love. We are just the *me* we are, but we are also God's *me*. The mystery deepens when we allow Spirit to be the reconciler of our accounts, be they failures or triumphs. The books are always kept out of our sight, thank goodness, and that frees us to live fully. We will not be judged by what we couldn't be or do. Letting ourselves be known through and through will reveal that love is the only true asset. The more we have of it, the more we can spend. It is the tender in tenderness. Can we then let reconciliation happen not by accounting but by trusting that we are enough as we are, beloved by God who declared us *good*? Then, as we do the tasks of caregiving as best we can, chinks may open in the automatic armor most of us have and allow care for us to seep into forgotten, invisible places. This is something that is surely off the books and under the table.

Here's another day to be aware,
to do the simple things that may help
another person to live in a better way.

This could just as easily be me
needing help.
We are all in constant change.

Let me look into my heart.
Let me look long and hard.
Am I giving care as an expression
of myself or as a way to avoid myself?
I know I can have a protective armor
that clanks with busy, busy, busy.

Let me daily reconcile my heart's truth.
Let me live another day of loving
with the love I have received.

Joy Training

We smile and clap when babies take their first steps. We coo and applaud when toddlers use a spoon getting food to their mouth instead of it landing on the floor. We love that they can hold their own cup, that they say Ma or Da for the first time. These are things to celebrate.

Perhaps we think there isn't much we can celebrate in declining years. It's hard to revel in the painstaking process of helping someone dress for the day. But with eyes of love we can be happy for them that they still can lift a leg into their trousers or a spoon to their mouths or that their hands can hold a cup. Can we celebrate the little miracles of self-care our charges can still manage? It can put a little joy into the day.

There are hospital and nursing home rooms where the atmosphere is very dreary and dark. Gloom Rooms. We know how we feel entering them for another day of keeping things going. But then there are, in the very same buildings, rooms where cheer is present. Those are the rooms where ways of reveling, joking, smiling, teasing, and loving are woven into the day no matter the difficulties at hand. Some people have joy-ceilings, invisible but solid glass over their heads. Somehow a feeling of joy can't penetrate those ceilings and open them with laughter or silliness. They may go through the motions, but the motions do not lift the heavy glass.

We know that to be grateful helps our days. In gratitude we see what is still possible, what can improve even just a little, and what can be accepted in old age and in illnesses of all sorts. The fine poet Wendell Berry, in one of his poems, reminds us that *"the impeded stream is the one that sings."* To revel is an expression of gratitude. It is possible in the midst of the trials and tribulations of giving care to be in joy. We are meant to have life and have it abundantly.

So why not celebrate for no special reason? It will help both caregivers and their charges. Can a little puppy or a baby come to visit and be enjoyed?

Wearing a costume to work, for instance, might bring a fleeting smile on the face of the ones we are caring for. Wrapping our charges in warm blankets and shawls to take them outside into the sun brings refreshment to us both. A sensual treat can be liberally slathering non-medicinal and lovely hand cream on hands and feet. They affirm we are living our days and not just moving through them with a dreary sense of waiting for the end. Small and generous, these signs of life lived for their own sakes become possible revels when limitations are constant. They are the tufts of grass growing through a crack in the pavement. A day lived with things like these makes it a good day in which joy is invited.

I forget my clown hat and
wear my frown instead—a mask of gloom.

Let me learn to accept the good,
the bad, and the boring,
and how all of it, in time, conspires
to become enlivened by joy.

Help me take my shoes off,
shed my scrubs and my apron.
Let me wear the out of doors
on my sleeves—the smell of snow,
the fragrant air, and the pungent earth.

Let me trust joy to be right here
even when things are tough.
I'll still hear the birds sing.

Tender Questions

Busy, busy, busy: there's no time to step back, to oversee and review our situations. Still, we can be concerned. Is what we have in place doing the job? What if anything needs change for our sake or for the sake of our charge? Is the environment pleasant for *all* involved? Is what we are giving of ourselves wanted, needed, in the way, or spot on? Are we appreciating the people we care for enough? Can we still see what they accomplished in life and who they deeply are? Do we know what matters to them at this stage in their healing or decline? Do we know what sustained them before and what can be of sustenance now?

What a heap of questions! Who has time for all this probing? It is so busy all the time that there is no time for discernment. But taking a time, set apart, to feel into what hovers close and is not listened to, is crucial and can make the difference between living a beautiful, though trying life versus merely enduring.

In the earlier reflection on refuge, having the thoughtful ear of someone professional was suggested. Such a person or friend can shape our questions and help us through a process of patient review so we can come to more clarity. Review should not be a process where we tell ourselves we're not doing a good job. It's not about being scolded and shamed into believing we are not aware or loving enough or neglecting what is needed. Review is not about judgment. It is more like a safety net to catch the pieces that might fall, the way a net may be under a trapeze artist. As caregivers, don't we often hang in midair by a thread? It's practical and a comfort to have a net under us.

With the help of someone or perhaps with careful journaling, we can ask those salient questions that have niggled us. We can better see where function is to follow being and not the other way around. Stumbling between immensities as we are, what is missing? For now, it's good to put thoughts about specific jobs, equipment, and services to one side. Are we focusing on finding out if there is anything loving and human that is missing? That's a tender question, and when we can answer that with fullness of heart, the other things that are needed will come clear, and we can act on them.

In review, can we shed our roles as caregivers and live more in the sanctity of an open-ended questioning process? Can there be more love here for everyone? Can we make that our main focus? To discern is a spiritual practice and one that is tender for all concerned.

I think I have to do so much all the time.
I think I'm not enough for the job.
The truth is I'm not.
The job is always bigger than I am.

Help me trust I am enough
as just plain me, and know that with others,
love will be present,
and therefore a sufficiency of help.

I already know that hiding in a role
hides my heart.

Help me shed that overcoat.
Let me find unity with You instead.

Help me see clearly
what is really needed.
Help me review.

Stark and True

A lovely thing to be about in our caregiving is to talk about the good memories we have of things that mattered in our lives, the events that are still vivid and full of goodness. There may be short-term memory loss, but the glow from some events from the past can still be felt.

As we encourage our loved ones to recall what pleased them from early on and what they are proud they once did, we'll also remember and benefit. It is a shared inner picture gallery, a retrospective. The temptation, of course, is to mostly recall the hurt. Life is always a mix where goodness and difficulty are blended. We don't really see something bright on a canvas without the needed dark outlines. It's the whole picture we want, isn't it? Suffering helps us see grace. Joy helps us notice what is not in joy as yet. It is finally all wonder...full. Reassured by Psalm 139, we are told *that the darkness and the light are both alike to God.*

What then of people with dementia, Alzheimer's disease, memory loss, and other delusionary states? What are we able to bring to them more than tenderness and acceptance? We will need it for ourselves big time, for we have already to a large extent lost the one we loved. We have lost them a little piece at a time. And when they become what we might call *someone else*, what then? We will be alone in our recollections. Those moments still mean the world to us, but they won't be shared. We'll have lost our common history, and there is deep loneliness in that.

The wrench of no longer being *with* each other is a deep wrench. So much can be borne if there still is a consciousness of the relationship over time. But if this is no longer so, how can we continue to care deeply? Most probably we can't. We will care differently. The face on the pillow is the face we have loved, but the person is gone into states we can't be part of. We must then care for our loss in quiet ways with people who remember us together back when.

Sometimes when we sing or play songs from the past, there can be a flicker of recognition in our loved one. But loss is loss, deep and wrenching, and no matter how many photos of *back then* we are able to look at, grief will be there as the companion we now have.

Stark and true as this may be, there is yet the task of holding a loved one's hand, washing their face, humming the familiar song that keeps us human. We are recollected into loving for its own sake, though not perhaps for the one who is there and no longer the person we once knew.

Loss is so stark.
I feel ripped from all that once mattered.
I feel disconnected from everything.

This territory is bleak and barren.
How do I live here?
How do I continue to love
when my love is no longer here?

Help me find a way
to come fully into my heart.
Let me still find fire
in the dark cave I am in.

Let me feel that Love itself is not missing,
that it is there in the dark waiting for me.
I want to recall
the good times and to feel
they are still here somehow,
and that Love remembers me
when I forget who I am.

Sleeves Rolled Up

Caregiving confirms something basic and life-giving in us. It both takes things away from us and returns us to a center of belonging with life, with ourselves and with those we care for.

Caregiving eventually strips us of the niggling need to feel certain. Little by little it takes away clinging to something that is ultimately not any sort of port in the storm. It replaces clinging with growing in presence and love, in acceptance of difficulty. It strengthens us by overcoming those difficulties. We are relieved of pretending we are something we are not. Fundamentally, our loving nature, our commitment, and our vulnerability reveal us. We are there in our plain and basic humanity. It means we have traded needing security for being present instead where we find ourselves. It is deeply knowing that we have a direction in life and a place to care.

Caring is always being renewed. We have a wellspring of meaning inside us through belonging and giving. The more we care, the more there is of care. It is a generous field without fences. It gives us stability, too, as we daily go about what we are about.

As persons we will always be unfinished, the way love is always unfinished, New and precious ways to live will always somehow be present. We need not fear the abundance of this. We are not asked to do more than we can from moment to moment. Love lived this way seems to unclutter and streamline our lives. There's a rhythm to it, and we see better what counts not only for our charges but for ourselves as well.

As we are streamlined by love, we give up more and more of what is irrelevant and discover the possibilities that are already present. This makes us creative in both small and significant ways, infusing more comfort and love for our charges. It will also surprise us with ways we never thought we could have imagined our lives. Caregiving has a way to order our lives and give them stability because we are needed by someone or by something. Therefore, we are invited into more expressive being. We are not talking about codependence and the insecurity of false giving but about something deeply of value.

These benefits all have the stark background of the day-by-day challenges and the love-tasks that present themselves. We are finding meaning in our lives with our sleeves rolled up and with a willingness to surrender personal safety and certainty for offered love and simple presence.

Help me become the one I really am.

Let me have a heart that participates.
Let me drop
what is no longer needed
and focus on what is truly needed.

*I know I won't be able to provide all
that is needed,, but with your grace
I can give what I can.*

*Accepting difficulty and loss
let me not shy away from life as it really is.
Help me accept both difficulty and loss.
I know that right here and now
there are possibilities for more engagement
and satisfaction.*

*Though it may be that those engagements
are small, let them renew me.
They are real
and can change things for the better.*

When Character Is Fate

When caring for another or for something important to us calls upon our true gifts we will feel a sense of destiny. We sense how we are aligned with and living *our* lives. We are somehow flowing with life itself no matter how hard the circumstances might be. We are becoming more of who we are in connection with another or something other, and so mysteriously are they. Our actualization is in tandem.

This can only happen when we understand our freedom to love the way we can, not the way we can't. When the need to be applauded, to be more than we are or do more than we can, or to please others has dropped away, we can sense that at some level we are growing. This becoming is internal. Maturity is developing the way a deep friendship might develop. Our direction in life is emerging from inside while taking our nature into account along with our particular gifts.

This may not mean that we will be hands-on caregivers. We may not have a natural gift for that, but we might find employment that makes use of our gifts and that will give us the resources to hire helpers whose gifts are doing the good hands-on tasks. We are then free to give our presence to the one in our care by simply spending time with them, listening and sharing a meal or a story.

Slowly, as we live this path of caregiving, we discover that we must take care of the path itself and be responsible for it. This goes beyond the persons we help. It is a vocation. When we realign with that vocation, we will understand that something of our nature chose it as a way for us. Character is fate, we have been told.

If we were astronauts we'd have to be trained. We'd have to be fit and understand what goes into a space flight or space walk. Up there, we'd experience the immensity of the universe, but we'd also have a real place next to our ship and to others who are working with us. When we align with care, it thrusts us into the unknown, into the vastness of life with a capital L. In that majesty we have our calling, our place, our work, and others to help us to keep the ship of our circumstances safe enough.

Because so much of hands-on caregiving is in the minutia of daily care: pills, diapers, showers, meals, dressing and undressing, enemas, laundry, etc., it is good to feel how immense the universe of care is. It is a huge, multi-dimensional world. Living our choice to serve in alignment with that spaciousness, there will be starlight. We will sense that we are walking in the vast space and immensity of love.

So much is about perspective.
I feel myopic here cleaning up
the bathroom again.

I know that everything small
is yet in majesty and that while wiping
the sink I am also in the stars—here
with running water and a rag.

Teach me to see
that whomever I care for
is in essence You.
Let that knowing complete me.

Patience

Growing into the inner freedom of caregiving that has been chosen is without doubt the work of a lifetime. As Ralph Waldo Emerson said, we should *adopt the pace of nature: her secret is patience*. Caregiving will shift our focus from one person to another, from one accepted objective to another. Always, when given from the heart, it will grant us a place in the world where we belong.

What riches are found in patience! It has the pace of kindness. It allows for maturing time and for mistakes. It works with our nature so that the love that has been placed in us can blossom. Experiencing the tenderness that patience bestows on us is a great comfort. No matter how heavy and thwarting a day of caregiving can be, there is also a depth of forgiveness and timelessness there. It is good to realize we will always be unfinished and growing.

Take the sea. It may be choppy with huge waves and stormy conditions on the surface, where sea spume hurls and spatters everywhere. But deep below the surface there is calm. That quality of patience can be ours if we would only allow ourselves to submerge into it.

It is patience that generates patience. That quality does not manipulate others, does not ask them to be other than who they are. It is actually a quiet state of gratitude for the *other*, since in truly being with them we become more of who we are. We are growing as we tend them. When we no longer force anything we grow at a suitable pace. We also stop being observers and become participants. That doesn't mean we stop noticing, but it does mean we have closed the distance created when we view someone to be *over there*, separate from us. We also shed the isolation that happens to us when we objectify others. We'll always know we are hip high in life together. Isn't it then that we receive what is given, which we did not have to be given in the first place and which we could not demand either? It is as if in embracing patience and being embraced by it, a tenderness arises that makes us gentle to both our charges and to ourselves.

Illness, continuous decline, depression, pain, and the feelings they generate are the daily encounters of caregiving. All of this will not go away, but it will inform us and transform us. We will more and more know that the task of caregiving is a holy task.

How do I do this day after day?
Without You I cannot get out of bed
to manage endless hours of care.

Your patience is timeless
and never stops.
It is there for me to feel,
and to be immersed in
before I even begin the tasks that need doing,
and the conscious presence I want to offer.

You hold my listlessness,
my sense of grief that my own life
is slipping by me as I do what
I feel called to do.

You dissolve my resistance
in the healing waters of Your patience.
I return to You.

I return to the deep place
where my life is
and where its meaning is unfolding,
and where your love is found.

A LAST WORD

There is no such thing as an assigned *fate* placing caregivers in the tough work they do. Their tasks are fraught with challenges, lack of appreciation, and as often as not, minimal resources. The work may have been thrust upon them by family need or other circumstances. They may find themselves in a *no choice* situation. Then the miracle is that they are nevertheless there.

With grit, with the gifts they have been given, and with God's grace bestowed on them, caregivers do their meaningful and holy work. Hopefully, they will come to know and feel that something far more has happened to them and in them. *The privilege of a lifetime is to become who we truly are*, said C.G. Jung. This discovery is the gift that lies at the heart of caregiving.

He who has a why
to live can bear
almost any how.

Friedrich Nietzsche